The Grace of Giving
The Practice of
Extravagant Generosity

Robert Schnase

ABINGDON PRESS
Nashville

The Grace of Giving:
The Practice of Extravagant Generosity
All rights reserved.

Originally appeared in *Five Practices of Fruitful Living* by Robert Schnase,
which was published by Abingdon Press in 2010.

ISBN 978-1-6308-8306-5

14 15 16 17 18 19 20 21 22 23--10 9 8 7 6 5 4 3 2 1
MANUFACTURED IN THE UNITED STATES OF AMERICA

Contents

The Grace of Giving
The Practice of Extravagant Generosity

They are to do good, to be rich in good works, generous, and ready to share, thus storing up for themselves the treasure of a good foundation for the future, so that they may take hold of the life that really is life.
—I Timothy 6: 18-19

The Fruitful Living Series

Jesus taught a way of life and invited people into a relationship with God that was vibrant, dynamic, and fruitful. He said, "I am the vine, you are the branches. Those who abide in me and I in them bear much fruit…. My father is glorified by this, that you bear much fruit and become my disciples," (John 15: 5, 8) Jesus wanted people to flourish.

Scripture is sprinkled with phrases that point to fruitful living—the kingdom of God, eternal life, immeasurable riches, a peace that passes all understanding, abundant life.

How do I cultivate a life that is abundant, fruitful, purposeful, and deep? What are the commitments, critical risks, and practices that open me to God's transforming grace and that help me discover the difference God intends for me to make in the world?

How do I live the fruitful, flourishing life of a follower of Christ?

Radical Hospitality. Passionate Worship. Intentional Faith Development. Risk-Taking Mission and Service. Extravagant Generosity.

Since the publication of *Five Practices of Fruitful Congregations,* these edgy, provocative, dangerous words have helped hundreds of congregations understand their mission, renew ministries, and stretch toward fruitfulness and excellence for the purposes of Christ.

The Fruitful Living Series moves the discussion of Christian practice from the congregational level to the personal practices of discipleship. The fruitful God-related life develops with intentional and repeated attention to five essential practices that are critical for our growth in Christ.

Radical Hospitality in our personal walk with Christ begins with an extraordinary receptivity to the grace of God. In distinctive and personal ways, we invite God into our hearts and make space for God in our lives. We receive God's love and offer it to others.

Through the practice of *Passionate Worship*, we learn to love God in return. We practice listening to God, allowing God to shape our hearts and minds through prayer, personal devotion, and community worship. We love God.

Through the practice of *Intentional Faith Development*, we do the soul work that connects us to others, immerses us in God's word, and positions us to grow in grace and mature in Christ. We learn in community.

The practice of *Risk-Taking Mission and Service* involves offering ourselves in purposeful service to others in need,

making a positive difference even at significant personal cost and inconvenience to our own lives. We serve.

Through the practice of *Extravagant Generosity*, we offer our material resources in a manner that supports the causes that transform life and relieve suffering and that enlarges the soul and sustains the spirit. We give back.

These five practices—to receive God's love, to love God in return, to grow in Christ, to serve others, and to give back—are so essential to growth in Christ and to the deepening of the Spiritual life that failure to attend to them, develop them, and deepen them with intentionality limits our capacity to live fruitfully and fully, to settle ourselves completely in God, and to become instruments of God's transforming grace. The adjectives—*radical, passionate, intentional, risk-taking,* and *extravagant*—provoke us out of complacency and remind us that these practices require more than haphazard, infrequent, and mediocre attention.

These practices open our heart—to God, to others, to a life that matters, a life rich with meaning, relationship, and contribution. They help us flourish.

Christian Practice

The ministry of Jesus is grounded in personal practices. Jesus' life is marked by prayer, solitude, worship, reflection, the study of scripture, conversation, community, serving, engagement with suffering, and generosity. These personal practices sustained a ministry that opened people to God's grace, transformed human hearts, and changed the circumstances of people in need.

Christian practices are those essential activities we repeat and deepen over time. They create openings for God's spirit to shape us. Practices are not simply principles we talk about; practices are something we do. They make our faith a tangible and visible part of daily life. We see them

done in the life of Jesus, and we do them until they become a way of life for us. We become instruments of God's grace and love.

Through practice, we open ourselves to grace and let ourselves be opened by grace. We follow Christ, step by step, day by day, again and again; and by these steps and through these days, we are changed, we become someone different, we become new creations in Christ.

The books in this series are based on the premise that by repeating and deepening certain fundamental practices, we cooperate with God in our own growth in Christ and participate with the Holy Spirit in our own spiritual maturation. The fundamental practices are rooted in scripture and derived from the clear imperatives of the life of Christ. This isn't a self-improvement, pull-yourself-up-by-your-own-bootstraps notion of how we grow in grace. It's not about trying harder, working longer, or striving more to achieve God's blessing.

The Christian life is a gift of God, an expression of God's grace in Christ, the result of an undeserved and unmerited offering of love toward us. Every step of the journey toward Christ is preceded by, made possible by, and sustained by the perfecting grace of God.

The fruitful life is cultivated by placing ourselves in the most advantageous places to see, receive, learn, and understand the love that has been offered in Christ.

How to Use *The Fruitful Living Series*

The Fruitful Living Series is deeply personal, and as such it is composed of stories—the experiences, hopes, doubts, good efforts, and false starts of people like you and me. Faith journeys are used to illustrate key points so as to encourage honest reflection and conversation. But the approach is not individualistic—only about me, my, and mine. Every experience embeds us more deeply in the community of Christ because it is in the presence of our sisters and brothers that our spirits are sustained, our hearts encouraged.

I pray for those who reach for these books searching for understanding about their own faith journeys, that it may stimulate them to deeper life in Christ. But I pray especially for those who have been handed these books and who open their pages reluctantly, that they may open themselves to the possibility that something in the stories and reflections

may cause them to think more deeply, pray more earnestly, and serve others in a more fruitful and satisfying way.

This series is experiential rather than systematic or dogmatic. It relies on the experiences of ordinary people who have been extraordinarily shaped by their relationship to God. None of us has the complete picture. Movement toward Christ is never a straight line, uninterrupted, obstacle free, totally consistent, predictable, and easily describable. There are no perfect accounts that capture everything that lies behind and no completely reliable maps that outline the future in one's faith journey. Soul work is hard, and following Christ is messy, challenging, joyous, scary, painful, sustaining, and frustratingly indescribable.

This *Fruitful Living Series* is about the everyday faith of everyday people seeking to listen for God, to love each other, to care for those in need, to embrace the stranger, to live the fruit of the spirit.

These books are practical. They are about what we do daily and intentionally, and about who we become because of how God uses what we do. They suggest a compass rather than map; a direction helpful for many diverse contexts rather than a specific step-by-step, how-to plan that fits only certain terrain.

Engage the material personally. Discover what you can learn about yourself, your relationship with God, your personal desires and internal resistances in the life of faith.

And read *The Fruitful Living Series* with others on the journey to Christ. Use it in house groups, adult Sunday school classes, a weeknight book study, or with your family. Resolve to deepen your own practices of faith. Pray for one another and support one another in Christ. Encourage church leaders and pastors to use the book in retreats, sermon series, or evening studies. These five books focus the essential work that forms disciples; by cultivating these practices in the lives of those reached by the community of faith, the congregation fulfills its mission

of making disciples of Jesus Christ for the transformation of the world.

As a pastor and bishop, I've been granted the privilege of witnessing people whose faith is immeasurably greater than my own, whose sacrifice more than I myself could ever bear, whose impact in the lives of others through their service is immeasurably more than mine, whose personal discipline, depth of spirit, and maturing in Christ is far ahead of anything I shall ever achieve or hope to receive, and whose generosity is so extraordinary that it humbles me completely. This book is about how we learn from their fruitfulness in Christ so that we cooperate with God in becoming what God created us to be.

My prayer for you and your congregation is that *The Fruitful Living Series* helps us all grow in grace and in the knowledge and love of God. May we be changed from the inside out so that we can transform the world for the purposes of Christ.

The Grace of Giving

THE GOOD YOU CAN DO

*Have you ever come on anything
quite like this extravagant generosity
of God, this deep, deep wisdom?*
—*Romans 11:33,* The Message

Giving helps us become what God wants us to be.

As a pastor, each year I preached on tithing and proportional giving in preparation for Consecration Sunday, the day members offer their annual pledges to support the church's ministry.

Before the service one year, Terri and Charles visited me in my office. Terri described what happened the previous year during the preparation for Consecration Sunday. In my sermon I said that giving is not merely about the church's need for money, but about the Christian's need to give. Afterward, she and Charles had a long, difficult conversation about the sermon. She poured out her heart about her unhappiness with the way they were living, and Charles agreed. "We couldn't breathe," she said. "We were living a lie. We had a big beautiful house, two cars, a boat, and everyone thought we were so happy. But underneath we were stressed out, arguing all the time about money, in debt over our heads, and we felt miserable. We were strangling."

Terri and Charles both had high-income, professional careers.

They earned plenty. "But we lived in constant fear," Terri said. "We were afraid of what others would think if we downsized our house or traded in our cars or stopped doing the things everyone else was doing. We were afraid of the bills, the debts, the banks. We were scared of what would happen if one of us became sick. We were afraid of the shame of bankruptcy. We were afraid our teenagers would find out how precarious our situation was. And we didn't talk about it for fear our marriage couldn't withstand the stress."

Terri was now wiping tears from her eyes as she continued the story. Last year, after the sermon they had talked honestly about all of this for the first time, and Terri had courageously said to Charles, "What kind of life does God really want us to have? Not this kind!" Thus began the journey a year before that had brought them to my

office that day. They finally faced what they had been avoiding. With prayer and courage, they had filled out last year's pledge card giving one percent of their expected income. When they offered it up to God, they sealed it with a commitment to start fresh in all things related to money. They read books, took a course, and consulted a professional. They spoke with their children and included them in a plan to turn their lives around. Some decisions were major—to move into a more modest neighborhood and to sell a high-payment car in order to buy a used one. They canceled credit cards. Like a team on a mission, the family dialed back expenses. They ate at home, repaired things themselves, and planned a modest vacation. They spent more time talking together as a family. They adopted a plan and adapted their lifestyle to live comfortably while paying off debt, saving money, and giving more. Charles said, "A year ago, we never imagined that we would feel the peace we feel today. It seemed totally beyond reach."

After finishing their story, Charles pulled from his pocket their pledge card for the upcoming Consecration Sunday, handed it to me, and said, "Pastor, it's not huge, but it represents two percent of our income for this next year. Our whole family is committed to watching that number grow year by year. All of us have signed the card, and when we offer it we will renew our commitment to God and to each other as a family. Giving has become a gift to us."

Giving

Through the practice of Radical Hospitality, we receive God and invite God's love into our lives. By practicing Passionate Worship

We love God in return; God shapes our hearts and minds as we begin to see the world through God's eyes. We cooperate with the Holy Spirit in our own spiritual growth as we practice Intentional Faith Development. God calls us to make a difference in the lives of others, and we practice

Risk-Taking Mission and Service. And at some point in our following of Christ, we realize all that we are comes from God and belongs to God; this leads us to the practice of Extravagant Generosity.

Hundreds of scriptural stories, parables, and verses focus on possessions, wealth, poverty, giving, gifts, offerings, tithes, charity, sacrifice, generosity, and sharing with those in need, providing a strong theological basis for giving.

In the Old Testament, people of faith practiced *first fruits,* the giving of the first and best of the harvest, livestock, or income for the purposes of God. Abram offered up a tithe, or tenth, of everything, and Jacob returned one-tenth of everything to God (Genesis 14:20; 28:22). The Psalms and Proverbs repeatedly encourage the sharing of gifts with God and with the poor. The prophet Malachi implores people to rely completely upon God, teaching them that when they practice the tithe they will find God's providence

and promise to be true (Malachi 3:8-10). Giving reveals and fosters trust in God.

Jesus teaches that the widow who dropped two coins in the temple treasury gave more than all the wealthier people because she, out of her poverty, gave all that she had (Luke 21:1-4). And he highlights the foolishness of the farmer who built bigger barns to contain his earthly possessions while neglecting those things that would make him rich toward God (Luke 12:16-21). With his story about Lazarus suffering at the front gate of the rich person's house, Jesus reveals God's disfavor with the wealthy who refuse to help those in need when they have the capacity to do so (Luke 16:19-31). How we use money matters to God.

"Giving, not getting, is the way. Generosity begets generosity" (Luke 6:38, *The Message*). Giving opens our souls to God's lead.

"For God so loved that world that he gave his only Son" (John 3:16). The root of generosity is God's love.

Paul says, "Have you ever come on anything quite like this extravagant generosity of God, this deep, deep wisdom? It's way over our heads. . . . Everything comes from him;/Everything happens through him;/Everything ends up in him" (Romans 11:33-36, The Message).

Paul writes, "You are familiar with the generosity of our Master, Jesus Christ. Rich as he was, he gave it all away for us – in one stroke he became poor and we became rich" (2 Corinthians 8:9, The Message). And Paul describes how the Christians at Macedonia gave not only according to their means but beyond their means, and then he pushes others to excel in their giving in the same way (2 Corinthians 8:3-6).

Where God's Spirit is present, people give.

John Wesley wrote extensively on the use of money, the danger of riches, and the importance of giving. For Wesley, all things belong to God. This changes how we perceive the manner by which we earn money and save money, causing us to do so in appropriate ways. And it changes how we spend money, making us more responsible, and shapes how we give money. Wesley valued industrious and productive work, but he believed that acquiring money does not provide a profound enough life purpose to sustain the human spirit. When he wrote, "Earn all you can, save all you can, and give all you can," he drew an unbreakable link between acquisition and generosity, inviting us to use our material wealth to deepen our relationship with God and to increase our positive impact for God's purposes.

ALL THE GOOD YOU CAN

Do all the good you can,

By all the means you can

In all the ways you can,

In all the places you can,

At all the times you can,

To all the people you can,

As long as ever you can.1

—John Wesley

No stories from Scripture tell of people living the God-related spiritual life while fostering a greedy, self-centered, self-serving attitude. Knowing God leads to generosity.

REFLECTION

"GIVING, *not* GETTING, *is the way.* GENEROSITY *begets* GENEROSITY"

—*Luke 6:38,* The Message

Giving helps us become what God wants us to be. Giving reveals and fosters trust in God.

Questions

- Who first taught you to give? Who modeled generosity for you?

- How are you continuing to learn to give?

- What motivates you to give?

- How does giving shape your relationship to God?

- In the chapter, John Wesley is quoted as saying, "Earn all you can, save all you can, and give all you can." What does this say to you? Where does it connect with your own goals and inspiration?

Prayer

Strengthen me, O God, for the hard work of being honest with myself as I seek to practice Christ-centered generosity.

WHY DO WE GIVE?

"Take care! Be on guard against all kinds of greed; for one's life does not consist in the abundance of possessions."
—Luke 12:15

Even with consistent teachings, many people wonder, Why become more generous? What difference does it make? How does something so material and mundane have anything to do with our spiritual lives? How does generosity help us flourish?

Giving Helps Congregations Thrive

Many people give simply because they love their church and they want the life-changing ministries of their congregation to prosper. They are themselves the beneficiaries of the church's ministries and they do their share to pay for the bills, the salaries, the facilities, and the costs so that the church can offer outreach, children's ministries, worship, and mission. They support the church so that others can receive what they have received. Their giving is functional and purposeful, a transaction that helps the church fulfill its mission and continue into the future. The fruit of this giving is tangible and visible; it is both immediate and long-term. Churches with

generous members offer more ministry, work with greater confidence, have less conflict, and make a greater impact on their communities and on the world. Responsibility and hope for the church motivate the giver. People want their congregations to thrive.

Giving Aligns Us With God's Purposes

People give because their contribution aligns with the purposes God wants them to fulfill in the world. Helping people, relieving suffering, teaching the spiritual life, reaching young people—when we sense God's call to make a difference, we can contribute our time or become personally involved in the day-to-day ministry. Another way to make a difference is through giving, contributing the resources that make possible the work that we feel called to support.

We please God by making the difference God wants us to make.

WHY WOULDN'T YOU DO IT?

Paul and Carolyn have been leaders in their congregation for years, and their generosity has grown steadily as they have matured in faith. They also have enjoyed substantial financial success. When their church felt called to reach more people and younger generations by building a new sanctuary, Paul and Carolyn were challenged to give a major gift. They prayed about it for weeks, before deciding to give the largest gift they had ever given in their lives. "I felt like I was asked to partner with God for a great purpose," Paul said. "Our gift became one of the great delights of our lives. We loved knowing that we could make a difference. We were deeply moved by the experience." Carolyn adds, "If God gives you the capacity and the passion to do something, why in God's name wouldn't you do it?"

Giving Changes Us Inside

People give because generosity helps them achieve God's purposes in *themselves*. By giving, we develop the inner qualities of generosity. Generosity is not a spiritual attribute someone acquires apart from the practice of giving. It becomes discernible only through visible behavior. We cannot become generous and cling to everything we have without letting go. The opposite of generosity is greediness, selfishness, self-centeredness, and self-absorption. These are not the qualities that lead to life, and so by our giving we cultivate a different nature inside ourselves.

God uses our practice of giving to reconfigure our interior life. By giving, we craft a different inner desire as the driving element of life. Our motivations change.

Giving moderates the powerful and sometimes destructively insatiable drive for acquisition. In the daily

interior struggle fostered by a consumerist, materialist society that pressures us to pursue many things that do not lead to real happiness, the practice of giving aims us at what ultimately satisfies. Giving sanctifies and deepens the struggle, and constantly resets the internal compass in the right direction. Generosity becomes a tool God uses to draw us closer to God and to align us more closely with God's desire for us.

Giving Mirrors God's Nature

We give because we are made in the image of God, whose essential nature is giving. We are created with God's nature imprinted on our souls; we are hard-wired to be social, compassionate, connected, loving, and generous. God's extravagant generosity is part of our essential nature as well. But we are anxious and fearful, influenced by a culture that makes us believe we never have enough. And we are scarred by habits that draw us away from God and

that turn us inward with a corrosive self-interest. God sent Jesus Christ to bring us back to ourselves, and back to God. As we "have in us the mind that was in Christ Jesus," we become free.

Giving Fosters a Healthier Relationship to Money

Giving puts us in a healthier relationship with our possessions, and with the material world in which we live. We like making money, but we enjoy other things as well, such as the love of our family; belong- ing to community; a sense of meaning, accomplishment, contribu- tion, and service. We enjoy making a positive difference in the lives of other people. But how do we maintain balance and perspective? How can we appropriately secure the basic needs of food, shelter, education, and health while also living with purpose? How do we avoid too much preoccupation with the things that do not ultimately

satisfy, and cultivate those things that do? The intentional practice of generosity helps us keep our priorities straight.

When asked how much money they would need to earn to be happy, people of all different incomes answer the same. If they could only earn about twenty percent more than they presently do, they would finally arrive at a satisfying happiness. Persons earning $10,000 dream of reaching $12,000; those earning $100,000 believe that with just $20,000 more per year they will be happy; and people earning $500,000 believe that when they earn $100,000 more they will finally arrive. We pursue a receding goal. This is a prescription for never-ending unhappiness. We can never possess enough to satiate the appetite for more. Single-minded pursuit of lifestyles highlighted by pop culture keeps us stuck on the surface of existence, captured in the material world, unhappy with what we possess, and blind to the real riches.

When we accept unreflectively the myths of money, we suffer from a self-created, culturally-fostered discontent. Forty-year-olds feel like failures because they are not millionaires; families buy houses beyond their capacity to afford; people pine for what they cannot possess. We wallow in abundance while suffering from a self-proclaimed scarcity. Despite the fact that we live in better houses, earn more money, drive nicer cars, spend more on entertainment, and enjoy greater conveniences than ninety percent of the world's population, or than we ourselves enjoyed thirty years ago, we never have enough.

Tolstoy, in *How Much Land Does a Man Need?* writes about a man, Pakhom, who farms the land given to him by his father. He want more, so he saves and sacrifices until he expands his acreage, and even this is not enough. He hears about another region where more land can be bought with less money, so he sells his farm and moves his family across the country to the larger spread. Still, he is dissatisfied.

Finally, he hears about a place where the king is offering an extraordinary deal. If you give the king all your money, you may take possession of all the land you can personally encompass by walking around in a single day. Pakhom imagines how far he could walk in a day, and all the land he could own. He sells all his property, travels to the new country, and pays the king in exchange for his chance to walk the perimeters of the land that will be his.

A stake is hammered into the ground before sunrise. Pakhom must return to the stake before sunset, and all the land that he circles before that time will be his. As the day dawns, he sets out. He runs at full speed in order to cover as much territory as possible. As the day heats up, he slows down and begins to circle back, but he sees lush pastures that he must possess, so he extends his path to include them. Late in the afternoon, he sees a stream that he cannot resist and so he enlarges his reach so this will be his. As the sun moves lower, he realizes that he has miscalculated, and

he fears that he may not return to his starting place in time. He runs harder to reach the stake before sunset, pushing himself beyond exhaustion.

He comes within view of his destination with only minutes to go. Pushing dangerously beyond his body's capacity to continue, he collapses and dies within reach of the stake.

How much land does a man need? Tolstoy ends his short story by saying that "six feet from head to heel" was all he needed.[2]

We are surrounded by inducements that make us acutely and painfully aware of what we lack, more so than of what we have. Without beliefs and intentional practices that counterbalance the influences of culture, we feel discontent no matter how much we have. Extravagant giving is a means of putting God first, a method for declaring to God and to ourselves the rightful order of priorities.

When we practice it, we live with a more relaxed posture about money, less panicked and reactive. We take possession instead of being possessed. Money becomes a servant rather than our master. By provoking us to give, God is not trying to take something from us; God is seeking to give something to us.

Every time we spend money, we make a statement about what we value. All inducements to spend money (advertising, social expectation, seeking to impress people) are attempts to shape our values. When we fail to conscientiously decide what we value and align our spending habits accordingly, a thousand other inducements and voices stand ready to define our values instead. Giving provides a spiritually healthy detachment from the most harmful influences of a materialist society, an emotional distance that is otherwise unattainable. Giving protects us from the pangs of greed.

Giving Encourages Intentionality

The practice of generosity opens us to deeper reflection and conversation about wealth and how it relates to purpose and happiness. Serious giving leads us to ask, What is our family's definition of success? How wealthy do we hope we, or our children, will be, and why? What motivates us as a household, and what matters most to our happiness? What will become of the wealth we accumulate? How much do we give, and why? What difference do we want to make in the world? How does giving influence our rela-tionship with God? What does Extravagant Generosity mean for us? For God? These and other questions can only be asked with authenticity when they are supported by the practice of giving. Giving fosters intentionality.

Giving Deepens Our Relationship With God

Giving assists us in our quest for God. We cannot "pay" our way to a closer relationship with God: whether giving aids us in our relationship with God or not depends upon our inner attitude. However, an unrestrained appetite for wealth or clinging too tightly to what we possess can hold us back and cause us paralysis in our following of Christ. Scripture reminds us that "the love of money is a root of all kinds of evil" (1 Timothy 6:10), and "it is easier for a camel to go through the eye of a needle than for a rich man to enter the kingdom of God" (Mark 10:25, NIV). The rich young ruler cannot relinquish his wealth and so he forfeits life with Christ (Luke 18:18-25), the farmer builds bigger barns to store his possessions while avoiding eternal priorities and he loses his soul (12:16-21), the wealthy person ignores the sufferings of Lazarus at his doorstep and finds himself

separated from God (16:19-31), the servant buries his talents instead of using them for his master and receives condemnation (19:12-26), and Ananias and Sapphira perish for their deceit that was motivated by their desire to keep their money (Acts 5).

Our clinging and coveting and hungering for wealth can obstruct our pathway to God and to the life God would have us enjoy. When unrestrained desire for material riches occupies the soul, there is little room left for God. Like Paul's assistant, Demas, we fall too much "in love with this present world," and we abandon Jesus' mission (2 Timothy 4:10). Greed impedes growth in Christ.

On the other hand, by giving generously, our beliefs and trust in God rise to tangible form. We become doers of the word and not hearers only. Giving makes following God real. We can live a God-related life or we can live without attention to God's presence and will. The God-related life

means our relationship with God influences all we do. When we seek to do the things God would have us do, including giving, our practice intensifies our love for the things God loves. Then the material possessions that can serve as a distraction or impediment to following Christ become an instrument for our serving Christ. They provide an opening, a way of following, a vocation. Finite things open our hearts to spiritual callings, and created things deepen our relationship with the creator. God's Spirit helps us become less attached to temporal possessions, and through the practice of giving, the same material things that might have tripped us up and turned us inward are used by the Spirit to carry us forward and to draw us outward. Our material goods, consecrated to God, nourish our desire to serve God. Generosity feeds our love for God.

Giving Honors Christ's Sacrifice

Finally, people practice generosity to honor the sacrifice of Jesus Christ. By giving extravagantly, we participate

in the ultimate self-giving nature we perceive in the life, death, and resurrection of Christ. Transformation involves dying partially to the things we love. God gives us life. Our return gift is the giving of our whole selves to God. We give because we have received.

REFLECTION

Speaking to the people, he went on,
"TAKE CARE!
Protect yourself against the least bit of
GREED.
Life is not defined by what you have,
EVEN WHEN YOU HAVE A LOT."

—Luke 12:15, The Message

> *God uses our practice of giving*
> *to reconfigure our interior life. By*
> *giving, we craft a different inner*
> *desire as the driving element of life.*
> *Our motivations change.*

Questions

- Do you sometimes feel that your life consists in the abundance of your possessions? Why?

- How can practicing generosity counteract greed and begin to balance the priorities of your life?

- Can you think of a time when giving and intentionally planning to give has given you a healthier relationship with money and material things?

- How does your giving to God influence other aspects of your life?

Prayer

I am your project, Lord. Use my desire to give to create me anew.
Never forget me, even when I forget you.

The Grace of Giving

CONTENTMENT AND GENEROSITY

I have learned to be content with whatever I have. I know what it is to have little, and I know what it is to have plenty . . .I can do all things through him who strengthens me.
--Philippians 4:11-13

The critical issue of ownership undergirds our theology of giving and stewardship. To whom do the material goods and wealth we enjoy ultimately belong? I'm not talking about the legal right of ownership, but rather a faith perspective—stewardship—that's rooted in thousands of years of Judeo-Christian theology and practice.

Fundamentally, we either consider the material things in our life—our money, house, property—as owned by God and belonging to God, and we manage them for God's purposes, or we view them as owned by us. If they are owned by God, then our tithes and offerings represent our returning to God what belongs to God already. What we keep also belongs to God, and we feel obligated to spend it wisely and not frivolously, and to invest it in ways that do not dishonor God's purposes. We try not to waste money or to live more lavishly than we should. We spend responsibly, allowing our relationship with God to form our minds. We manage God's resources as faithfully as we can.

But if we believe that our material resources fundamentally belong to us and that we entirely possess them ourselves, then we can do whatever we please with what we own, and our tithes and offerings are giving something that belongs to us, to God. God should be grateful for our generosity in giving a percentage for God's purposes rather than our feeling grateful for the privilege of using what belongs to God.

Which of these two views do we hold? Which perception is truest? Do the things of this life come from us, belong to us, and end with us?

For example, think about the possession of land. Suppose we hold legal title and own land according to civil authorities. In the larger span of the earth's history, does our patch of soil actually belong to us, or are we temporary stewards? The land didn't begin with us and doesn't end with us. The land we claim to own has existed for millions of years, was used by humans for millennia before us,

and will remain for eons more after we are gone. For the ordering of civil life, we rightly say we own the property and it belongs to us. But our mortality assures that we are only the temporary stewards, managers, and keepers. At our dying, what will the things we own mean to us? Whose will they be? People live and perish, but purposes are eternal. With that understanding comes a profound and humble sense of responsibility about how we use the land. It's temporarily ours to enjoy, but we do so with respect and awe, because ultimately everything belongs to God, and not to us.

This concrete example applies to all of the temporal elements of our lives—our possessions, our wealth, even our bodies and minds. Which perspective is truer, more ethically sound, more aligned with reality? That it all belongs to us and we can do whatever we want? Or that we are the temporary beneficiaries, and we find meaning in using what God has entrusted to us to the highest purposes? Which perspective fosters better decisions and

deepens a spiritually grounded sense of community and responsibility? The wisdom revealed in Scripture and tradition for more than three thousand years is that those who practice from the perspective of a steward find greater happiness.

Contentment

Generosity derives from a profound reorientation in our thinking about how we find contentment in life. Paul writes, "I have learned to be content with whatever I have" (Philippians 4:11). Paul was not a slacker, lacking in initiative! He was industrious, competitive, and ambitious for the work of God. Paul also realized how seductive our activity and our appetite for more could become. We begin to believe that happiness depends upon outward circumstance, visible achievements, and material com-forts rather than deriving from inner spiritual qualities—love, peace, compassion, self-control, gentleness, prayerfulness.

Even possessing greater wealth and finer houses than most of the world does not mean that we experience contentedness. We can still feel panic, emptiness, striving, and isolation. When we base our self-worth on our salary, or on which neighborhood we live in, or on what type of car we drive, then we race for more "meaning" by having more possessions. We feel needy, and our appetites become insatiable. Surrounded by water, we are dying of thirst. Feelings of scarcity paralyze us.

Breaking the cycle of conditioned discontent requires courageous soul work. It takes knowledge, insight, and the support of others to handle this from deep inside. The inner life shapes how we feel, what we value, and our attitude toward possessions. Contentment arises from seeking that which satisfies.

Abundant living derives from generative relationships, from mutual support, and from knowing how to love and

WHAT HAPPENS TO GOD'S LOVE?

> If you see some brother or sister in need and have the means to do something about it but turn a cold shoulder and do nothing, what happens to God's love? It disappears. . . . My dear children, let's not just talk about love; let's practice real love. This is the only way we'll know we're living truly, living in God's reality."
> —1 John 3:17-19, *The Message*

be loved. Flourishing results from a sense of purpose, of connection, of hope, of contribution. Contentedness comes from personal integrity, a life aligned with high values, depth of spirit and of mind, growth in grace and peace. These grant release from agitation, from unhealthy striving, and from continual dissatisfaction. Founded on these, we may value many of the things our culture induces us to seek, but without the harmful, destructive intensity. We want to improve our conditions and standing, but we don't

embrace these objectives with the panicked intensity our society would have us do.

Primarily, contentedness is formed in us by the practice of generosity. Contentedness is learning to be happy with what we have rather than feeling distressed by what we lack. In our voluntarily giving away part of our wealth and earnings, we are saying, "I can spend all of this on myself, but I choose not to." In that simple act, repeated and deepened with frequency and intentionality, we break the bonds of self-destructive acquisitiveness. We can do it; we are free to choose! Contentedness comes with living beyond selfishness and egotism.

Second, contentedness results from a deep, cultivated sense of gratitude. Generous people are thankful. They perceive the gift-like quality in everyday tasks and ordinary friendships, and in common experiences and little treasures. They realize that the best things in life come

gift-like, unearned, from beyond themselves, and are not created by them, but received by them. They give thanks in all things, and their gratefulness sharpens their awareness of the deeper sources of happiness. Their treasures are real and close and permanent, and unassailable by changes in the stock market. They give thanks for family, friendship, food, breath, the dawn of a new day, and for life itself. All is grace upon grace.

And contentedness results from the spiritual awareness that God has already provided us everything we need to flourish. We have enough; our income and home are sufficient. With sufficiency comes release from worry. Living more simply (and spending *below* our means rather than *beyond* our means) provides a countercultural path to greater peace. Sufficiency causes us to focus on what we *have* rather than upon what we *lack.* It keeps us from living in homes we cannot afford, driving cars whose payments overstress us, and taking jobs that disrupt our families

and undermine other values we hold. Asking questions of sufficiency makes us clearer about what we really *need* in contrast to what we want or what our culture *says we need*. Living more simply and reflectively and intentionally, we thrive.

Finally, contentedness comes from persistent interior work and cooperation with the Holy Spirit to develop the personal habits that keep us from surrendering our sense of well-being, identity, and purpose to materialist measures. We are not always accurate at forecasting what will make us happy, or what will provide us increased well-being rather than a temporary boost. Living fruit- fully is not merely a matter of having something *to live on,* but something *to live for.* Purpose, connection, love, service, friendship, family, generosity—these sustain contentedness.

The Tithe

For hundreds of generations, the practice of tithing has sustained growth in personal generosity. To tithe means to give a tenth, and involves returning to God ten percent of income. It's simple, concise, and consistent. Write down your income for the month, move the decimal point over one place, and write a check to the church for the amount you see. Do it first thing when you are paid, and you discover that the practice dials down appetites, reshapes priorities, and that all other expenses, needs, and savings will re- adjust. What could be easier?

I heard someone say that the first time he wrote a tithe check, it felt like he'd swallowed an avocado pit! For most people, tithing is not easy. It takes time to learn and adapt and grow into the practice.

MUSCLE MEMORY

Sarah grew up in a family that practiced tithing, and as a child she put ten cents in the offering plate from each dollar she received. She remembers receiving her first paycheck of $56 from her first job as a teenager, and her sense of achievement and delight when she gave $5.60 to the church. Now in her forties, Sarah has a high-paying job as a senior executive, and tithing continues to feel natural, a regular pattern of her life. She does it with ease and grace. "I love giving," she says, "and I cannot imagine living my life or loving God without giving back. Giving is one of the great joys of my life. Tithing was learned and practiced so early that I developed the 'muscle memory' for giving. Like practicing my tennis serve for so many years that I don't have to think about each step, my giving is part of who I am." For someone beginning to tithe, Sarah's level of discipleship may appear unachievable. But with practice, anyone can develop "muscle memory."

Some people perceive the tithe to be nothing more than a leftover from an Old Testament law-based theology. They believe it is an arbitrary, technical rule with little relevance for later periods.

And yet Jesus commended the practice, even among the Pharisees whom he criticized for making a show of their self-righteousness. The early church practiced the tithe, and so have Christians in every generation since. John Wesley tithed and expected early Methodists to give regularly and generously at every class meeting and chapel service. Their gifts were meticulously recorded so that people could hold themselves accountable to the practice of giving.

The people whom we admire and respect for their generous spirits, spiritual wisdom, and deep-heartedness invariably have practiced giving in such an extravagant manner that it has reshaped them. God has used their long-term patterns of giving to form in them the spiritual

qualities that cause them to be our mentors. They give extravagantly according to their means, and many beyond their means, and most practice or exceed the tithe. The tithe remains a basic expectation of discipleship.

Name one person you admire and respect because of all they keep for themselves. Name someone you consider generous and spiritually mature who never gives, or who constantly complains about giving, or who always seeks to give the least amount required. Largeness of spirit leads to an eagerness to give our utmost and highest.

Tithing provides a consistent and universal baseline, a theologically and biblically faithful standard, that is nominal enough to allow people of nearly any income to meet without imposing great hardship and yet large enough to stretch us and to cause us to do the necessary reordering of our priorities that spiritually reconfigures our values.

Tithing provides a concrete way for us to take the words we speak, "God is Lord of my life," and put them into practice. Our commitment becomes tangible; our giving becomes a way of putting God first, an outward sign of an inner spiritual alignment.

Tithing challenges us to ask ourselves, Is my giving generous? Or merely expedient? Do I give for practical reasons to help the church, or for spiritual reasons to nourish my spirit?

Tithing is not merely about what God wants us to do, but about the kind of person God wants us to become. Does the giving I now practice help me develop a Christ-like heart?

Tithing requires honest prayer. What would God have me do? Are there things God would want me to give up in order to tithe? Many people have tithed even in

the face of adversity, and have felt blessed doing so. The practice causes us to adapt our behaviors to someone else's will: God's. Tithing is not merely a financial decision; it is a life choice that rearranges all the furniture of our interior lives. That's why we do it.

One hundred and fifty years ago, our great-grandparents tithed if they were active people of faith. Why did they find it possible to tithe back then when we have trouble tithing today? Was it because they were so much wealthier than we are today? Absolutely not.

The opposite is true. We have trouble tithing today because we give in more affluent times, and we have allowed our affluence to shape us more than our faith.

If you are new to faith and the prospect of giving ten percent appears overwhelming, take time to grow into the practice over a few years. Give proportionately— a set percentage of income, such as one or two or five—

until you mature to the tithe. If you are facing unusual hardship, overwhelming debt, the loss of employment, or some other adversity, give as you are able during this season. But as stability returns, move toward the tithe in small incremental steps. With practice, tithing becomes easier, more natural. It will change your life.

On the other hand, if you have been an active follower of Christ and a member of a congregation for twenty, thirty, forty or more years, and you have discovered the grace and love of God, participated in worship, matured through Bible study, and offered yourself in mission, and all these have provided for you a sustaining faith, but you do not tithe, then prayerfully consider why this particular spiritual practice does not apply to you? Why have you avoided this practice while embracing all the others? What makes this practice the exception? What makes you the exception?

REFLECTION

Let's not just talk about
LOVE; *let's practice*
REAL LOVE.

This is the only way we'll know we're
LIVING TRULY, *living in*
GOD'S REALITY."

—*1 John 3:18-19,* The Message

And contentedness results from the spiritual awareness that God has already provided us everything we need to flourish. We have enough.

Questions

- How do you feel about the statement "all things belong to God"?
- What causes you to feel content?
- Think about someone who you admire for their generosity of spirit and giving. What do you see in this person that you would like to see in yourself?
- How do you avoid a self-destructive acquisitiveness?
- How do you feel about tithing? Do you practice proportional giving or tithing? If so, why? If not, why not?
- What's the largest gift you have ever given in your life?
- What motivated you? What resulted from the gift, and how did it affect you?

Prayer

Help me seek you above all things, to offer my best, to be rich in helping others, and to be as extravagantly generous with you as you are with me.

GROWING IN THE GRACE OF GIVING

*This most generous God who gives
seed to the farmer that becomes bread
for your meals is more than extravagant
with you. He gives you something
you can then give away, which grows
into full-formed lives, robust in God,
wealthy in every way, so that you can
be generous in every way. . . .*
—*2 Corinthians 9:11,* The Message

Why do we sometimes find it difficult to give generously?

First, fear stops us from giving generously. We fear we may have to give up things that give us pleasure. And yet, plenty of people live happily and fruitfully who earn ten percent less than we do. Once basic needs are provided for, there is no correlation between income and happiness. But there is a strong relationship between giving and joy. Greed lessens joy; generosity increases it. That's as true as gravity. Ironically, fear and greed are what we most need to moderate in order to live happily, and the practice of generosity is the most potent antidote.

Second, people underestimate the spiritual work and practical planning required in order to take giving seriously. They innocently think that if they attend church, study the Bible, sing in the choir, and volunteer on service projects, that they will somehow absorb automatically a more profound commitment to generous giving. This is

not true. Extravagant Generosity requires focused work, deep conviction, a mature spirit, learning, practice, and extraordinary intentionality. No one tithes accidentally. No one incidentally happens to leave an estate that rebuilds a congregation. Extravagant giving does not just happen.

Third, people convince themselves that they will tithe when they finally get a financial break that frees them to be generous, such as a large bonus, a promotion, a windfall inheritance, or winning the lottery. In fact, people tend to become less generous as they become wealthier. People who cannot find the spiritual courage to give from a lesser income are unlikely to find it easier to contribute from a greater income.

Fourth, some people feel called personally to give generously, but they do not receive support in their commitment from other family members. Don't you wonder what Zacchaeus's wife had to say when he arrived

home and shared with her what he had said to Jesus that day (Luke 19)? Was she angry, bitter, resentful? Or had she been longing for the day when Zacchaeus would come to his senses and return to his best self?

Finally, some people feel that money and wealth are simply not appropriate topics for spiritual reflection and teaching. They divide their spiritual lives from what they do with financial matters. And yet Jesus frequently addressed wealth as a matter of faith. Greed, charity, saving, inheritance, riches, treasure, giving, wealth, poverty, taxes, sharing—these are all topics of faithful exploration. Jesus embeds our faith in the gritty details of hard decisions made daily at work and home.

Despite the outward challenges, the inner struggles, and the countercultural nature of generosity, where there is a desire to give, there is a way. The two coins dropped in the treasury from the hands of the poor widow, noticed by

Jesus and recorded for all time as a model of Extravagant Generosity, forever reminds us that there is always a way.

The Practice of Extravagant Generosity

The practice of Extravagant Generosity stretches us to offer our utmost and highest to God rather than to give in a manner that is haphazard, unplanned, reactive, minimalist, mediocre, or mechanical. People who practice Extravagant Generosity give with unexpected liberality; they make giving a first priority; and they plan their giving with great energy and passion. They go the second mile. They do not give from a "what remains" mentality, but from a "what comes first" priority. Giving seriously becomes a personal spiritual discipline, a way of serving God, and a means of helping the church fulfill its God-appointed mission. Focused conviction and intention causes them to give in a more pronounced way, without fear and with greater trust. Giving changes their lives.

Extravagant does not correspond with giving that is merely dutiful, required, burdensome, mandated, or simply doing one's part. *Extravagant* denotes a style and attitude of giving that is unexpectedly joyous, without predetermined limits, from the heart, extraordinary, over-the-top, and propelled by great passion. *Extravagant* is the generosity seen in those who appreciate the beauty of giving, the awe and joy of making a difference for the purposes of Christ. Extravagant Generosity is giving to God as God has given to us.

People who practice Extravagant Generosity change their lives in order to become more generous. They shift things around so that they can do more. Their generosity opens them to projects they never dreamed God would involve them in! They become rich in giving.

They support ministries marked by fruitfulness and excellence, and they expect accountability and transparency.

They are conscientious and intentional. Generosity is their calling. They want their giving to make a difference. They care.

They grow in the grace of giving. They learn. They take small steps until tithing becomes natural. They deepen their understanding of giving through prayer and Scripture, and they foster generosity in others. They give more now than in the past and will give more in the future than they do today.

They push their congregations to become more generous, focusing more of their resources beyond their walls through mission and service. They advocate outward-focused ministry.

People who practice Extravagant Generosity do not wait to be asked. When they see a need, they step forward to meet it, offering their resources as a means of help.

They never expect to be catered to or begged by other church leaders to do their share. They do not give to control the church but to support it. They excel in giving. They love to give.

They give extravagantly with conviction. They are motivated by a desire to make a difference rather than by guilt, fear, desire for recognition, or to manipulate others. They give with humility.

And yet, they are willing to serve as an example to motivate others, to teach and lead and bear witness to the power of giving. They draw others toward generosity and toward God.

They teach their children and grandchildren to give, mentoring them by example on how to earn honestly, save carefully, spend prudently, and give lavishly.

They not only give out of present income, but occasionally they give from investments for major projects. When appropriate, they leave a portion of their estate for the church through their will. Their giving outlives them.

They look at difficult financial times through the eyes of faith rather than of fear. They persist in doing good. They give in all seasons.

They view personal success as a reason to share.

They enjoy giving. They pray and hope and dream about the good they accomplish through their gifts. They consecrate their giving to God. They delight in generosity.

They accept appreciation graciously when it comes, but they do not pine for acknowledgment or thanks. They give expecting nothing in return.

People who practice Extravagant Generosity learn to enjoy things without possessing them, to moderate their acquisitiveness, and to find satisfaction in simpler things. They avoid personal debt as much as possible. They save. They avoid overindulgence, ostentation, and waste. Their possessions do not rule them. They aspire, like Paul, to know the secret of being content with what they have.

They live with a sense of gratitude. They give thanks in all circumstances. Love is a gift, and life is grace.

They give generously beyond their church, contributing to causes that strengthen community, relieve suffering, prevent diseases, and make for a better future. They change lives. Their giving knows no bounds.

They delight in receiving money, find pleasure in its responsible use, and experience joy in giving it to God's purposes. They do not become too attached, and are not

stopped, deceived, slowed, misled, or detoured in their following Christ by the possession of money. They are rich toward God.

As If For the Very First Time

Charles Frazier, in his novel of the American Civil War, *Cold Mountain*, introduces a minor character, a fiddler whose life is changed through an incident that causes him to look at his musical talents in a whole new way.

The fiddler is a drunk, who plays only for drink, and he knows only six songs. His military unit camps near a house where there's a powerful explosion. A young girl is severely burned in the explosion and is near death, and her father sends for a fiddler to help ease her way to heaven. The fiddler doesn't know what to do; he's afraid, and enters the dark cabin where the young girl suffers in excruciating pain. From her deathbed, she says, "Play me something."

He plays a tune. "Play me another." The fiddler plays his drinking tunes slowly, thinking it more appropriate to the circumstances. Soon he has exhausted his small repertoire.

"Play me another," she says as she struggles against the pain. "Don't know no more," he says. "That's pitiful," she says, "what kind of fiddler are you? Make up a tune then." He marvels at such a strange request. It had never entered his mind to try such a thing. But he has a go at it. Soon the girl passes away. Her father thanks the fiddler for lifting her to heaven with his fiddle.

A transformation takes place, and the author writes, "time and time again during the walk back to camp he stopped and looked at his fiddle as if for the very first time. He had never before thought of trying to improve his playing, but now it seemed worthwhile to go at every tune . . . ."[3] Thereafter, he never tired of trying to improve at his playing, and he went into taverns of every kind to study the sounds and methods of other musicians.

He learned more than nine hundred tunes, and composed many of them himself. "From that day . . . on, music came more and more into his mind. . . . His playing was as easy as a man drawing breath, yet with utter conviction in its centrality to a life worth claiming."[4]

Picture him looking at his fiddle as if for the very first time, realizing that he can change lives with it and that he can lift souls to heaven. Imagine the difference he made in the lives of people and the meaning that was added to his own life. That ordinary fiddle and the simple gift of music, when used for higher purposes, became sacred. When he discovered the gift he had been given, and the power of that gift to influence the world for good, he was changed.

Before his incident with the girl, it had never occurred to him to want to improve but now with new purpose, he couldn't get enough of his gift of music. His ordinary talent became beautiful, a source of joy and meaning.

We find something similar through the practice of Extravagant Generosity. Giving causes life. Before, our giving may have been arbitrary, perfunctory, haphazard, a little here and there. But when we discover the great difference generosity makes; place it in service to God; and use our resources to relieve suffering, strengthen communities, and restore relationships, then we look at giving entirely differently. We look at our giving, and see it as if for the very first time. We discover that something as ordinary as our giving can help lift souls to heaven and change lives for the purposes of Christ. We want to improve on our generosity at every turn until it becomes as easy as drawing breath.

Through our generosity, God can do extraordinary things. Through our giving, God changes lives, and in changing them, transforms us.

REFLECTION

TELL THOSE RICH IN THIS WORLD'S WEALTH *to quit being so full of themselves and so obsessed with money, which is here today and gone tomorrow.*

TELL THEM TO GO AFTER GOD, *who piles on all the riches we could ever manage—to do good, to be rich in helping others, to be extravagantly generous.*

If they do that, THEY'LL BUILD A TREASURY THAT WILL LAST, *gaining life that is truly life.*

—*1 Timothy 6:17-19,* The Message

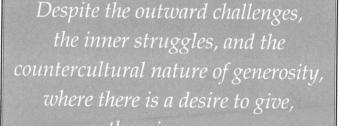

Despite the outward challenges, the inner struggles, and the countercultural nature of generosity, where there is a desire to give, there is a way.

Questions

- What obstacles prevent you from giving extravagantly?

- When was a time you felt God's Spirit move you to give your resources beyond what you had previously practiced?

- What's the most fun you ever had giving?

- What personal habits help keep you grounded in Christ? How has the habit of giving changed the kind of person you are?

Prayer

What a wildly wonderful world, God. All that I have comes from beyond myself. Open my heart, receiving and giving, like breathing in and breathing out.

Leader Helps
for Small Group Sessions

The Grace of Giving

Focus Point: The root of generosity is God's love. Knowing God and experiencing God's love lead to generosity.

GETTING READY *(Prior to the Session)*

Preparation:
• Read Chapter 1 in The Grace of Giving.
• Write the key Scripture and focus points on a board or chart.
• Review Digging In and Making Application, and select the pointss and discussion questions you will cover.
• Acquire a box of index cards and a bag of pens.
• Pray for the session and for your group members.

Key Scripture: *Have you ever come on anything quite like this extravagant generosity of God, this deep, deep wisdom? Romans 11:33 (The Message)*

Main Ideas:
• The root of generosity is God's love. Knowing God and experiencing God's love lead to generosity.
• Giving helps us to become what God wants us to be.

GETTING STARTED

Opening Prayer:
Lord, we acknowledge that you are Creator of heaven and earth, and that all things come from you. Help us to give all we can and live from a place of generosity as you call us to. Amen.

DIGGING IN

Note that the root of generosity is God's love, and that because of God's great love for us, God has been extravagantly generous on our behalf. Have several participants read aloud the following Scriptures: John 3:16; Romans 11:33-36; and 2 Corinthians 8:9.
Group Discussion
• How has God been generous on your behalf?
• How has God been generous to you personally?

Read aloud the excerpt from Chapter 1, "No stories from Scripture tell of people living the God-related spiritual life while fostering a greedy, self-centered, self-serving attitude. Knowing God leads to generosity."

The Practice of Extravagant Generosity

Group Discussion
• Does knowing and experiencing God's love and generosity motivate you to give? Explain your response.
• How does giving shape your relationship with God?

Review together the story of Terri and Charles from Chapter 1.
Group Discussion
• How would you describe Terri and Charles' life before they began the journey to change their lifestyle so that they could pay off debt, save, and give more? How would you describe their life after?
• What were some of the specific decisions and changes they made along the way?
• Why do we feel the need to try to keep up with what everyone else has?
• What would happen if all Christians got their financial situations in order and gave generously to the ministries of the Church?

MAKING APPLICATION

What Does It Look Like?
Read aloud the John Wesley passage, "All the Good You Can."
Briefly discuss
• How can we begin to practice this kind of generosity?

Hand out note cards and pens to each participant. Ask them to write the following questions along with their answers on their note cards. These answers will not be shared, but encourage them to keep this card in their Bibles or books and bring them each week as they will add to the list.
• Are you in a position to be generous?
• What needs to change about your situation to free you to be more generous?

What Now?
•Instruct participants to reflect silently in response to this question:
• In light of all we have shared today, what do you sense God saying to you?

End by inviting answers to these questions:
• In response, what will you do differently this week?
• How will what you learned this week change how you live your life?

Close your session with prayer requests and invite a participant to close in prayer.

The Grace of Giving

SESSION 2: *Why Do We Give?*

Focus Point: Generosity helps us to flourish by aligning with God's purposes, changing us inside, mirroring God's nature, and deepning our relationship with God.

GETTING READY *(Prior to the Session)*

Key Scripture: *Take care! Be on guard against all kinds of greed; for one's life does not consist in the abundance of possessions. Luke 12:15*

Main Ideas:
• Generosity helps us to flourish by aligning us with God's purposes.
• Every time we spend money, we make a statement about what we value.
• We cannot become generous and cling to everything we have without letting go.

GETTING STARTED

Opening Prayer:
Lord, we acknowledge that you are Creator of heaven and earth, and that all things come from you. Help us to give all we can and live from a place of generosity as you call us to. Amen.

DIGGING IN

Direct participants' attention to the reading for the week. Briefly review the ways that generosity helps us to flourish.

Group Discussion
• What difference has the practice of giving made in your life?
• What does it mean to be "aligned" to God's purposes?
• How does giving intensify our love for the things God loves? What are some examples of this?
• How have you seen people change as they became more generous givers?

Ask someone to read aloud the two-paragraph excerpt beginning, "People give because generosity helps them achieve God's purposes in themselves" (p. 33).

Group Discussion
• How do we develop the inner qualities of generosity?
• Why can't we gain the spiritual attribute of generosity without giving?
• What does it mean for God to reconfigure our interior life through our giving?
• In what ways do our motivations change as God reconfigures our interior life?
• Refer to the story from Tolstoy called How Much Land Does a Man Need?

Group Discussion
• Why is the pull of "more, more, more" so powerful in our culture?
• How difficult is it to overcome? Why?

MAKING APPLICATION

What Does It Look Like?
Review the story of Paul and Carolyn in Why Wouldn't You Do It?
Briefly discuss:
• When have you been asked to partner with God for a great purpose?
• When was the last time you considered that giving generously is a partnership with God?
• What passion and capacity has God given you?

Wrap up the session by reading aloud the final paragraph of Chapter 2.

Ask participants to pull out their note cards from last week. Ask them to write two new questions along with their answers on their note cards. These answers will not be shared, but encourage them to keep this card in their Bibles or books and bring them each week as they will add to the list.
• What is God speaking to about your aptitude for generosity?
• To what thing or things might you be called to giving generously?

What Now?
Instruct participants to reflect silently in response to this question:
• In light of all we have shared today, what do you sense God saying to you?

End by inviting answers to these questions:
• In response, what will you do differently this week?
• How will what you learned this week change how you live your life?

Close your session with prayer requests and invite a participant to close in prayer.

SESSION 3: *Contentment and Generosity*

Focus Point: The realization that all that we are comes from God and belongs to God leads us to the practice of Extravagant Generosity..

GETTING READY *(Prior to the Session)*

Key Scripture: *I have learned to be content with whatever I have. I know what it is to have little, and I know what it is to have plenty....I can do all things through him who strengthens me." Philippians 4: 11-13*

Main Ideas:
- The realization that all that we are comes from God and belongs to God leads us to the practice of Extravagant Generosity and undergirds our theology of giving.
- Generosity results from a reorientation in our thinking about how we find contentment in life.
- Tithing is a way of putting God first; it is an outward sign of an inner spiritual alignment.

GETTING STARTED

Opening Prayer
Lord, we acknowledge that you are Creator of heaven and earth, and that all things come from you. Help us to give all we can and live from a place of generosity as you call us to. Amen.

DIGGING IN

Have someone read aloud Romans 11:33-36. Then review together the two-paragraph excerpt beginning, "Fundamentally, we either consider the material things..."(p.50).
Group Discussion
- Which of these two views is truest? How close are you to living out the first view?

Now call attention to the example of the possession of land, "Think about the possession of land. Suppose we hold legal title and own land according to civil authorities..."
Group Discussion
- Does the idea that you are a temporary beneficiary motivate you to use what God has entrusted to you to the highest purposes? Why or why not?
- How can this perspective help us to make better decisions and deepen our spiritual sense of community and responsibility?
- Tell about a time when operating from the perspective of a "steward" (as opposed to an "owner") gave you a sense of satisfaction, fulfillment, or happiness.

The Practice of Extravagant Generosity

MAKING APPLICATION
What Does It Look Like?
Remind the group that tithing is a way of putting God first; it is an outward sign of an inner spiritual alignment. Point out that Jesus commended the practice, and that the early church practiced the tithe—as Christians in every generation since. Then read these statements from Chapter 3:

- Tithing provides a concrete way for us to take the words we speak, God is Lord of my life,' and put them into practice. Our commitment becomes tangible; our giving becomes a way of putting God first, an out- ward sign of an inner spiritual alignment."
- "Tithing is not merely a financial decision; it is a life choice that rearranges all the furniture of our interior lives."
- "We have trouble tithing today because we live in more affluent times, and we have allowed our affluence to shape us more than our faith."

Briefly discuss
- How do you feel about tithing? Do you practice proportional giving or tithing? Why or why not?
- When was a time you felt God's Spirit move you to give your resources beyond what you had previously practiced?

Wrap up discussion by reading aloud the four ways that contentedness is formed in us:
- The practice of generosity
- A deep, cultivated sense of gratitude
- The spiritual awareness that God has provided all we need
- Persistent interior work and cooperation with the Holy Spirit

Ask participants to pull out their note cards from last week. Ask them to write two new questions along with their answers on their note cards. These answers will not be shared, but encourage them to keep this card in their Bibles or books and bring them each week as they will add to the list.
- How difficult is it for you to choose to give rather than merely acquire? How is giving a part of your life?
- How successful are you in living within your means? How might you live more simply?

What Now?
Instruct participants to reflect silently in response to this question:
- In light of all we have shared today, what do you sense God saying to you?

End by inviting answers to these questions:
- In response, what will you do differently this week?
- How will what you learned this week change how you live your life?

Close your session with prayer requests and invite a participant to close in prayer.

The Grace of Giving

SESSION 4: *Growing in the Grace of Giving*
Focus Point: The practice of Extravagant Generosity stretches us to offer our utmost and highest to God rather than to give in a manner that is haphazard, unplanned, reactive, minimalist, mediocre, or mechanical.

GETTING READY *(Prior to the Session)*

Key Scripture: *This most generous God who gives seed to the farmer that becomes bread for your meals is more than extravagant with you. He gives you something you can then give away, which grows into full-formed lives, robust in God, wealthy in every way, so that you can be generous in every way. . . . 2 Corinthians 9:11, The Message*

Main Ideas:
• The practice of Extravagant Generosity stretches us to offer our utmost and highest to God.
• People who practice Extravagant Generosity give with unexpected liberality; they make giving a first priority; and they plan their giving with great energy and passion.
• People who practice Extravagant Generosity change their lives in order to become more generous.

GETTING STARTED

Opening Prayer
Lord, we acknowledge that you are Creator of heaven and earth, and that all things come from you. Help us to give all we can and live from a place of generosity as you call us to. Amen.

DIGGING IN

Direct participants to Chapter 4 to the section called The Practice of Extravagant Generosity. List together the habits or characteristics of people who practice Extravagant Generosity.
Group Discussion
• Why do you think these habits are critical to Extravagant Generosity?
• Which habits are more challenging for you, and why?

Acknowledge that there are many obstacles or resistances to Extravagant Generosity discussed in the chapter.

Group Discussion
• Which obstacles resonated with you?
• What other obstacles stand in the way of extravagant generosity?
• What would help you overcome those obstacles?

MAKING APPLICATION

What Does It Look Like?
Refer to story of the fiddler from the reading.
Briefly discuss:
• When have you seen God do extraordinary things through someone?
• How can our giving lift others toward heaven?

Invite participants to pull out their note cards from last week. Ask them to write two new questions along with their answers on their note cards. These answers will not be shared, but encourage them to keep this card in their Bibles or books and review them from time to time.
• What is "extravagant" about your current approach to giving?
• What patterns of giving do I hope God will use to reshape my life? How will I begin these patterns/practices?

What Now?
Instruct participants to reflect silently in response to this question:
• In light of all we have shared today, what do you sense God saying to you?

End by inviting answers to these questions:
• In response to these sessions on Extravagant Generosity what will you do differently this week?
• How will what you learned this week and in the book The Grace of Giving: The Practice of Extravagant Generosity, change how you live your life?

Close your session with prayer requests and invite a participant to close in prayer.

Notes

1 This quote is attributed to John Wesley.

2 Leo Tolstoy, *How Much Land Does a Man Need? and Other Stories* (Penguin, 1993); p.110.

3. Charles Frazier, *Cold Mountain* (Atlantic Monthly Press, 1997); p. 232.

4. Frazier; p. 232, 234.

The Grace of Giving
The Practice of
Extravagant Generosity

They are to do good, to be rich in good works, generous, and ready to share, thus storing up for themselves the treasure of a good foundation for the future, so that they may take hold of the life that really is life. —I Timothy 6: 18-19